Dedication

To Father God for giving me this awesome first book to share with families all over the world.
You are truly GOOD all the time.

I would like to say thank you to my family. I love you all dearly.

To all the people who sowed the word of God into my life, I say thank you.

To all the children I had the honor to share God's word with: You have truly blessed my life.

Written by Londa Presley
Illustrated and designed by J. Cecil Anderson

The ABCs of the Holy Bible, ISBN 978-0-615-37502-1

Holy Child Publications • P.O. Box 954 • Fairburn, Georgia 30213
Manufactured in the U.S.A.

**This book was designed for parent/mentor involvement.
For best use, review and paraphrase scripture references for children.**

Red Dot•Best Spot™ Page Numbering is a numbering method that utilizes a red dot icon, to serve as a counting aid and guide for young readers when turning book pages. This extends reading enjoyment through proper book care and preservation.

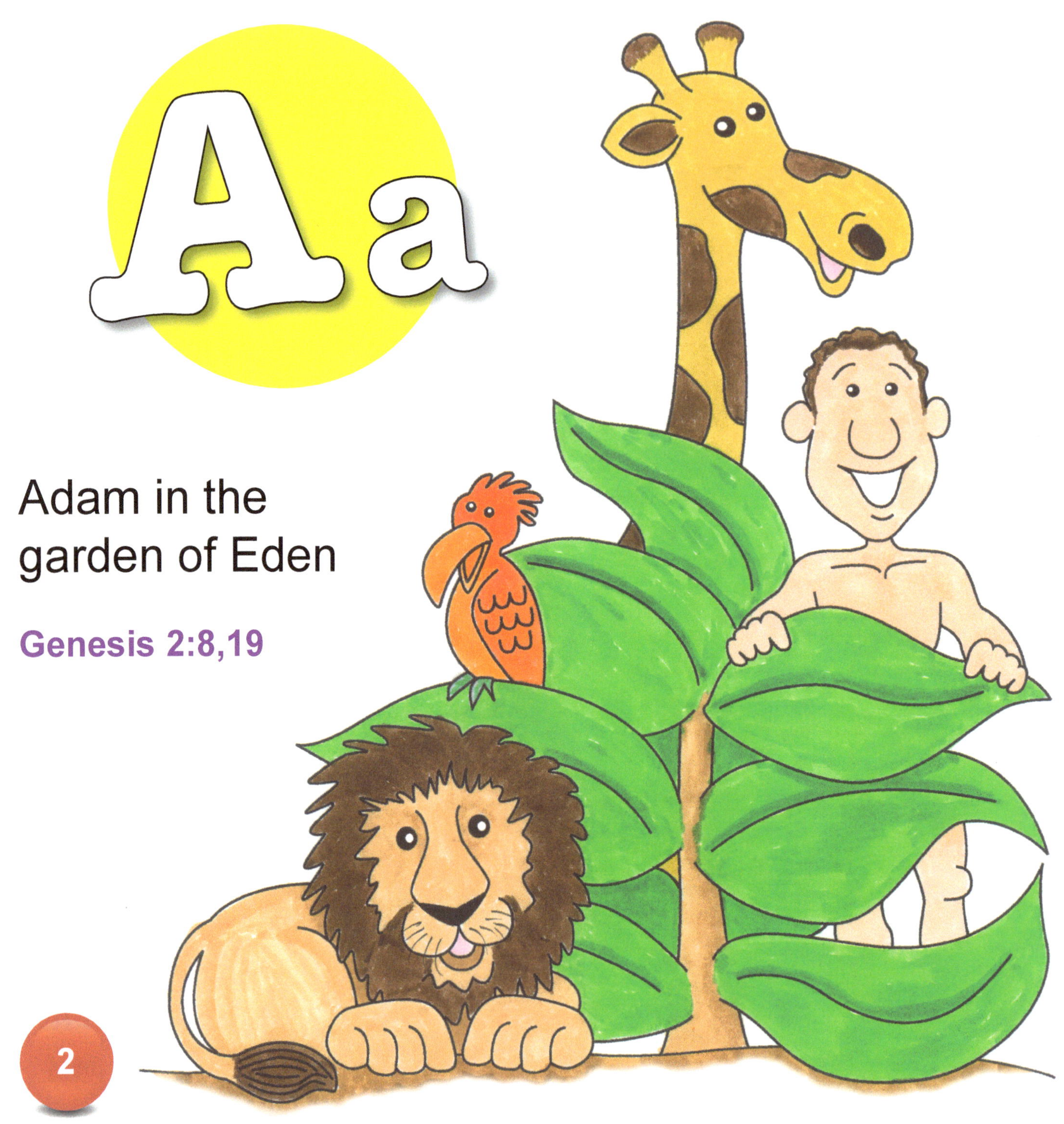
Aa
Adam in the
garden of Eden
Genesis 2:8,19
2

Baby Jesus
in a manger
Luke 2:7
Bb
3

Cc
Christ Jesus on
the cross
Mark 15:25,26,37
4

Daniel in the lion's den

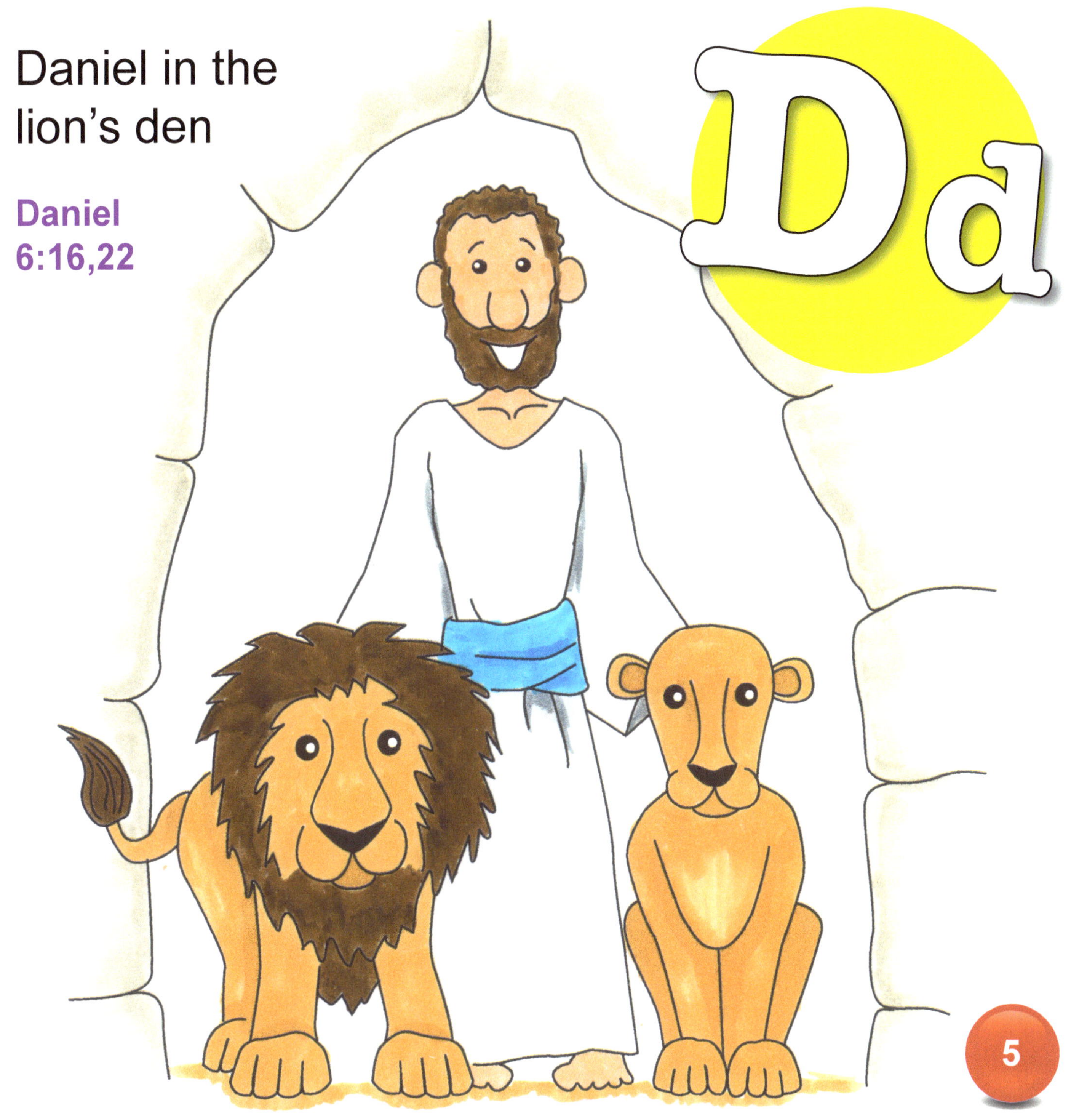

6

Elijah calls down fire   1 Kings 18:36-38

F f
Five smooth stones are what David chooses to fight Goliath
1 Samuel 17:40
7

God's creation

Genesis 1:31

8

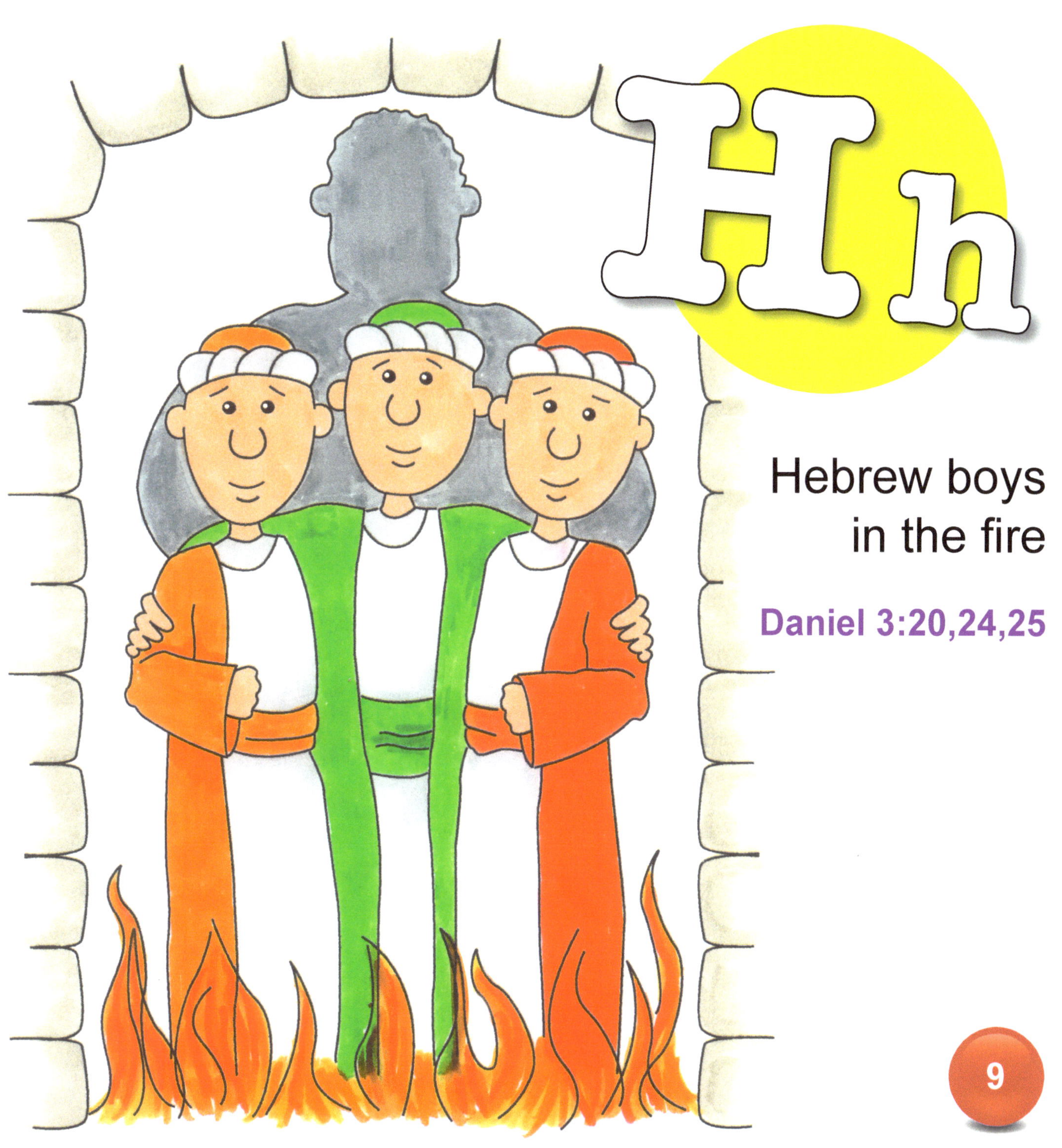

H h
Hebrew boys
in the fire

Daniel 3:20,24,25

9

Isaac, the son of promise

Genesis 22:13

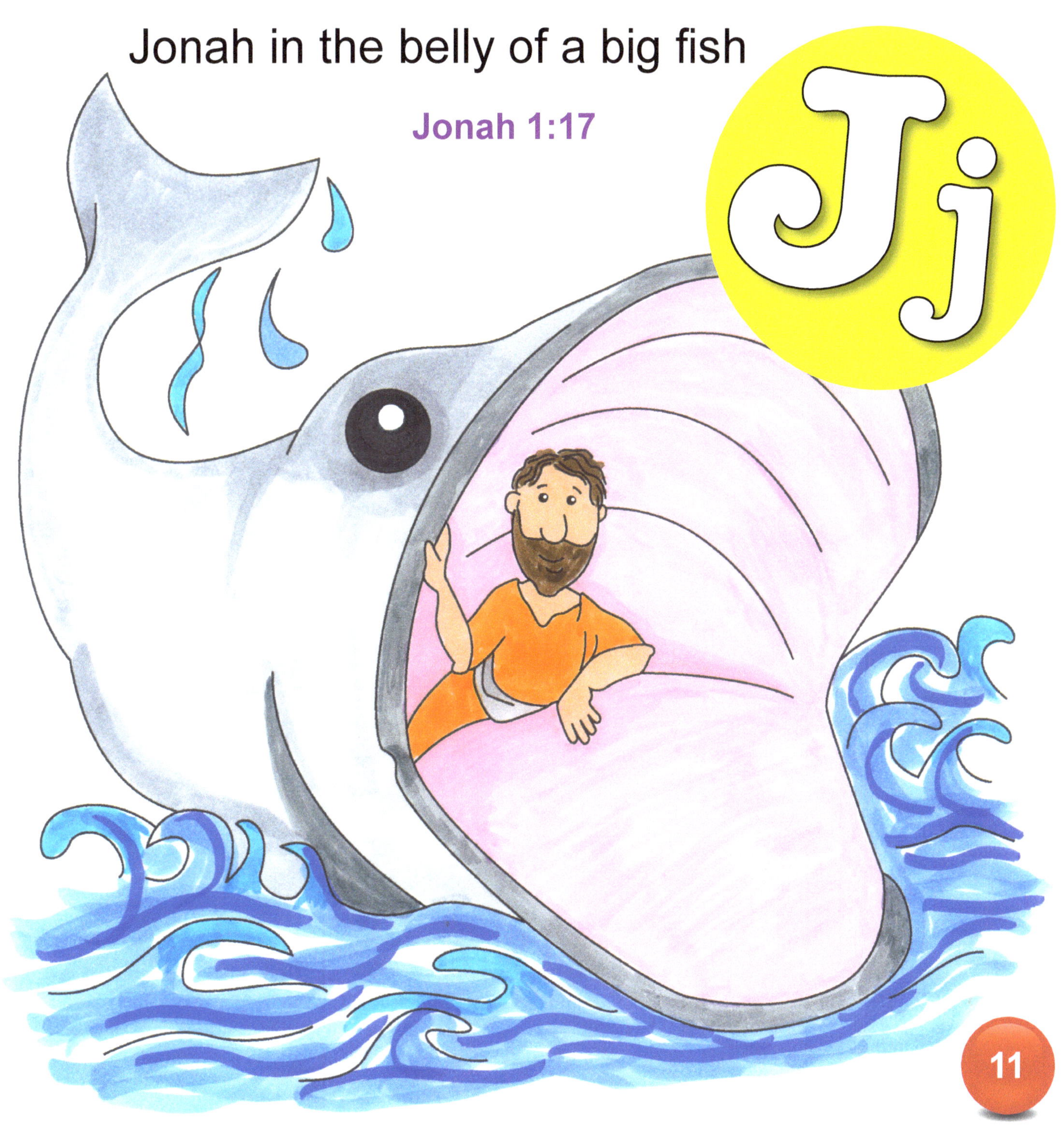

Jonah in the belly of a big fish
Jonah 1:17
Jj
11

K k

King Solomon
has wisdom

1 Kings 3:11,12,28

12

L l
Lazarus is alive
John 11:43,44
13

Moses parts the Red Sea

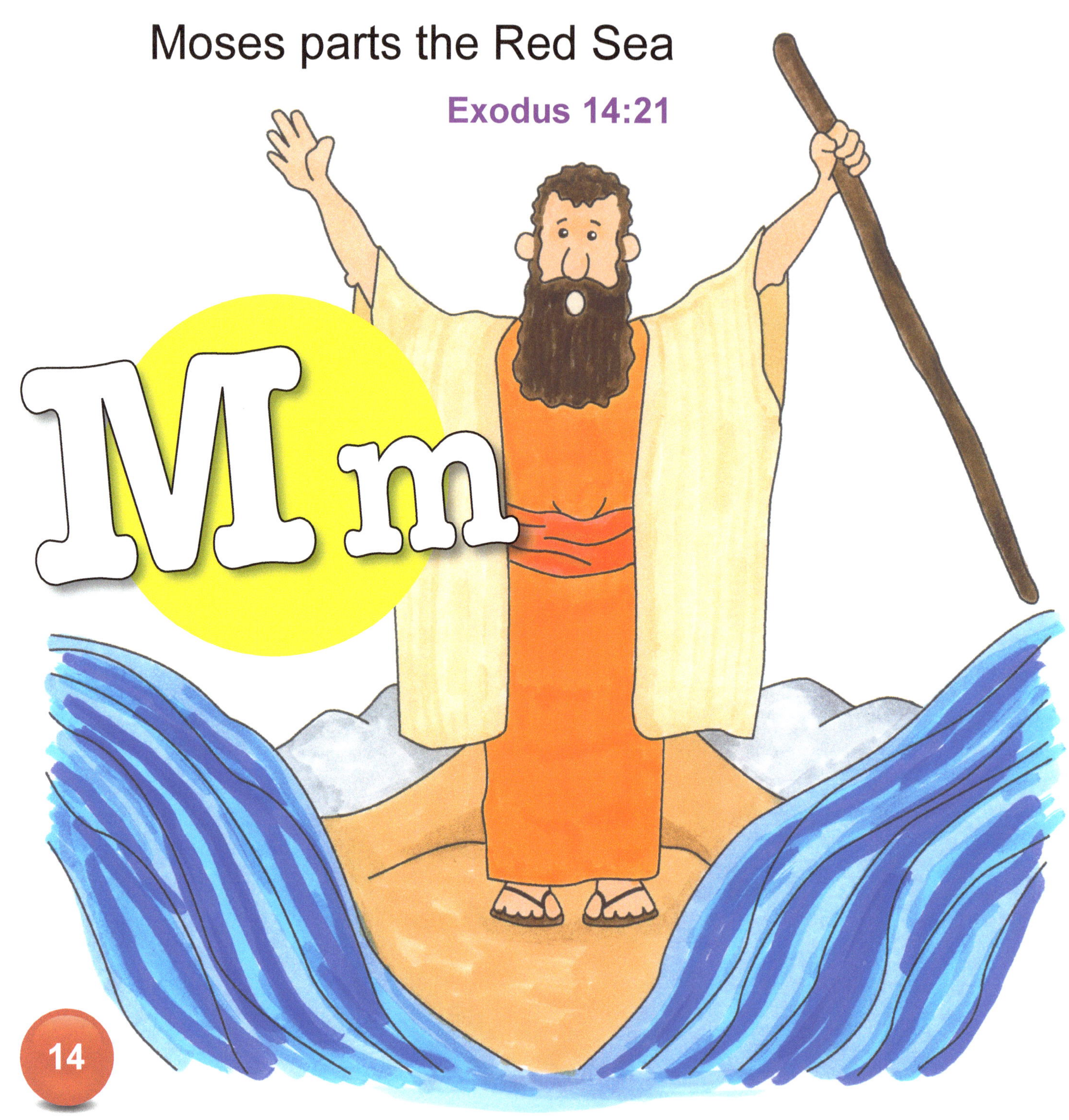

Noah builds an ark

Genesis 7:1-3

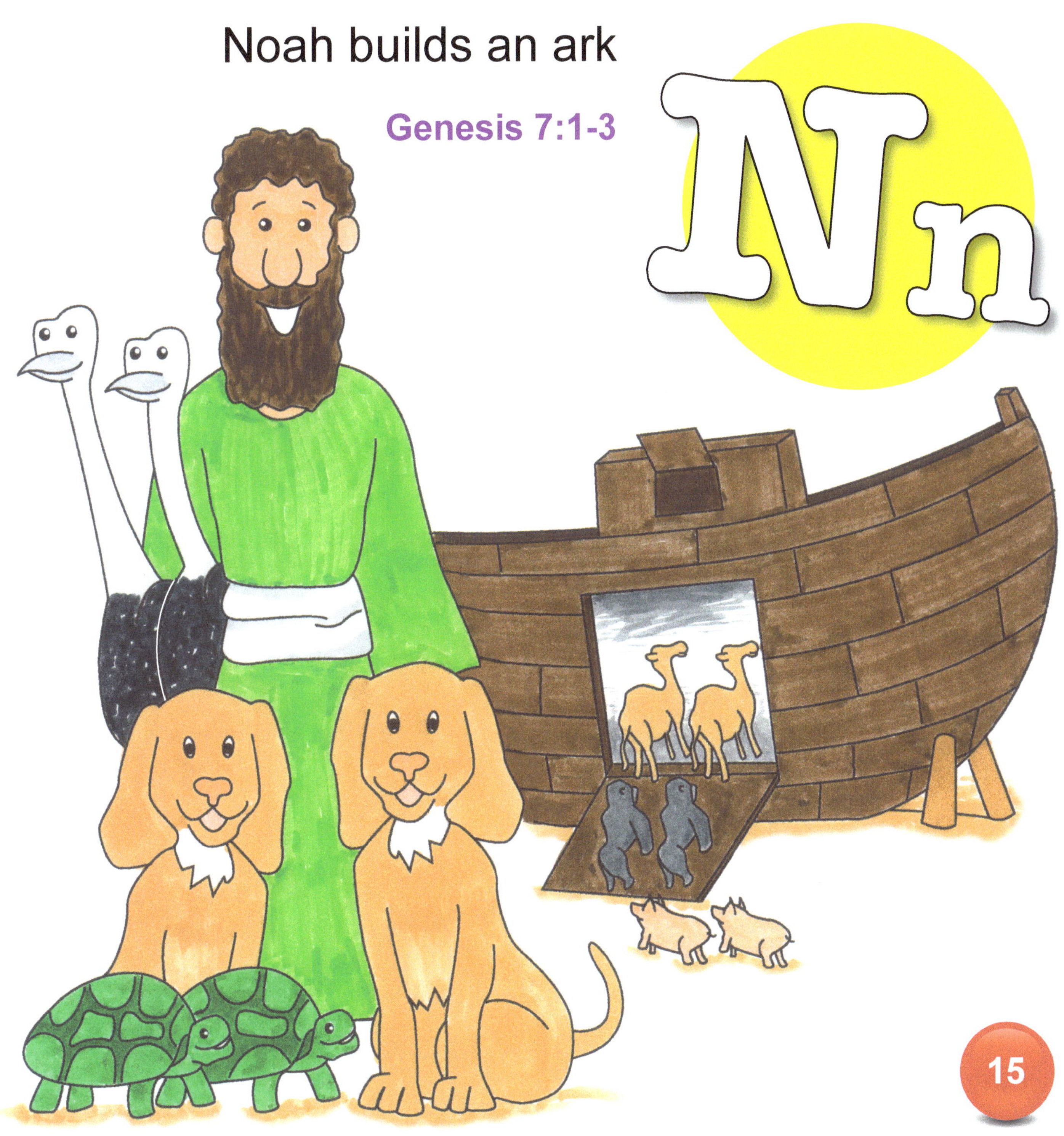

O o

Onesimus
returns home

Philemon 1:10-12

16

Pp
Peter finds money
in a fish's mouth
Matthew 17:24-27
17

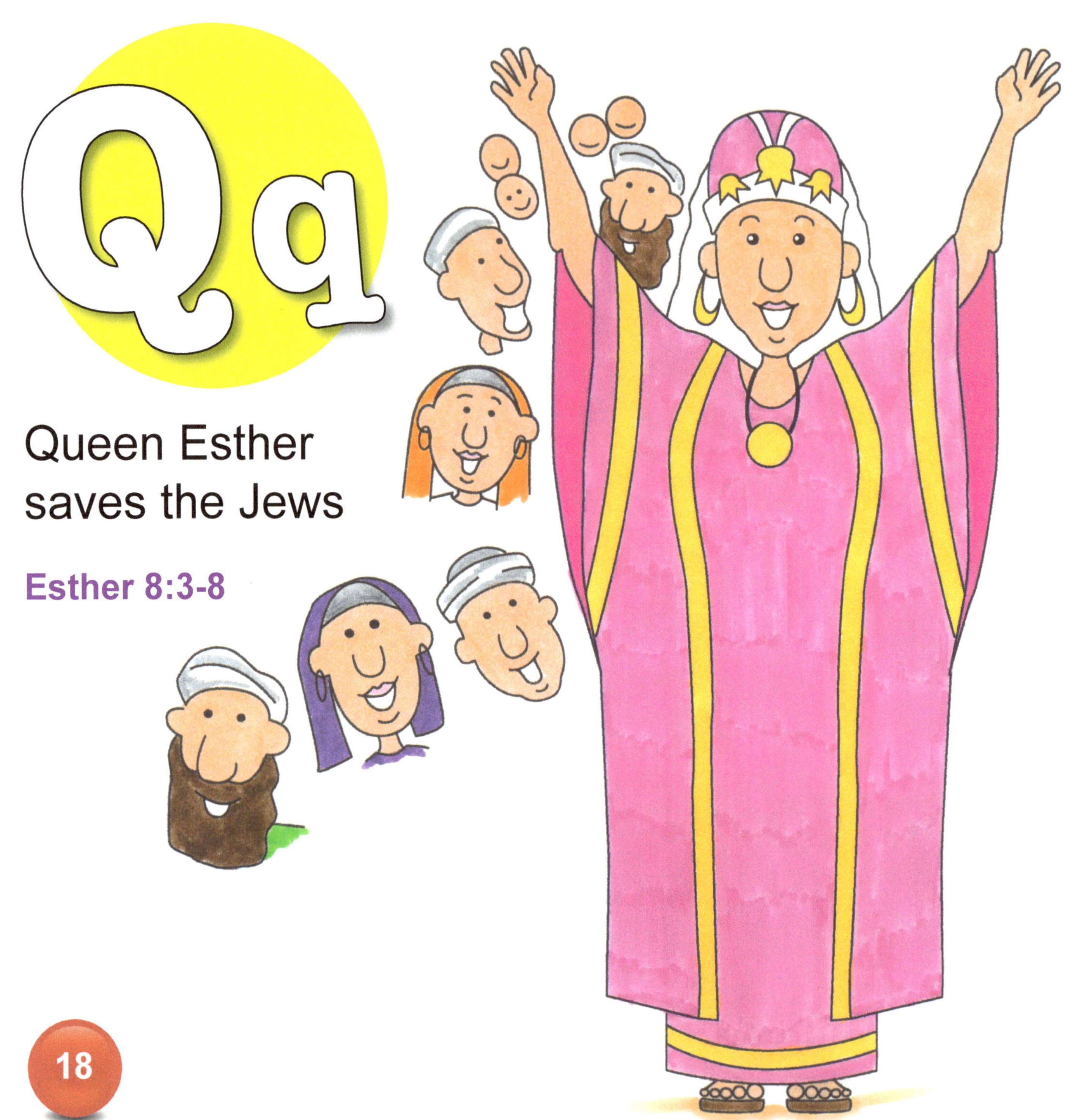

Qq

Queen Esther
saves the Jews

Esther 8:3-8

18

R r
Rahab helps
the spies
Joshua 2:15
19

Samson and Delilah

Thomas does
not believe
John 20:24,26,27
21

Ur is the city where Abraham was born

Genesis 11:27-31

22

Vineyard of
Naboth that
King Ahab
wants

1 Kings 21:1-3

23

Ww
Water turns into wine
John 2:7-9
24

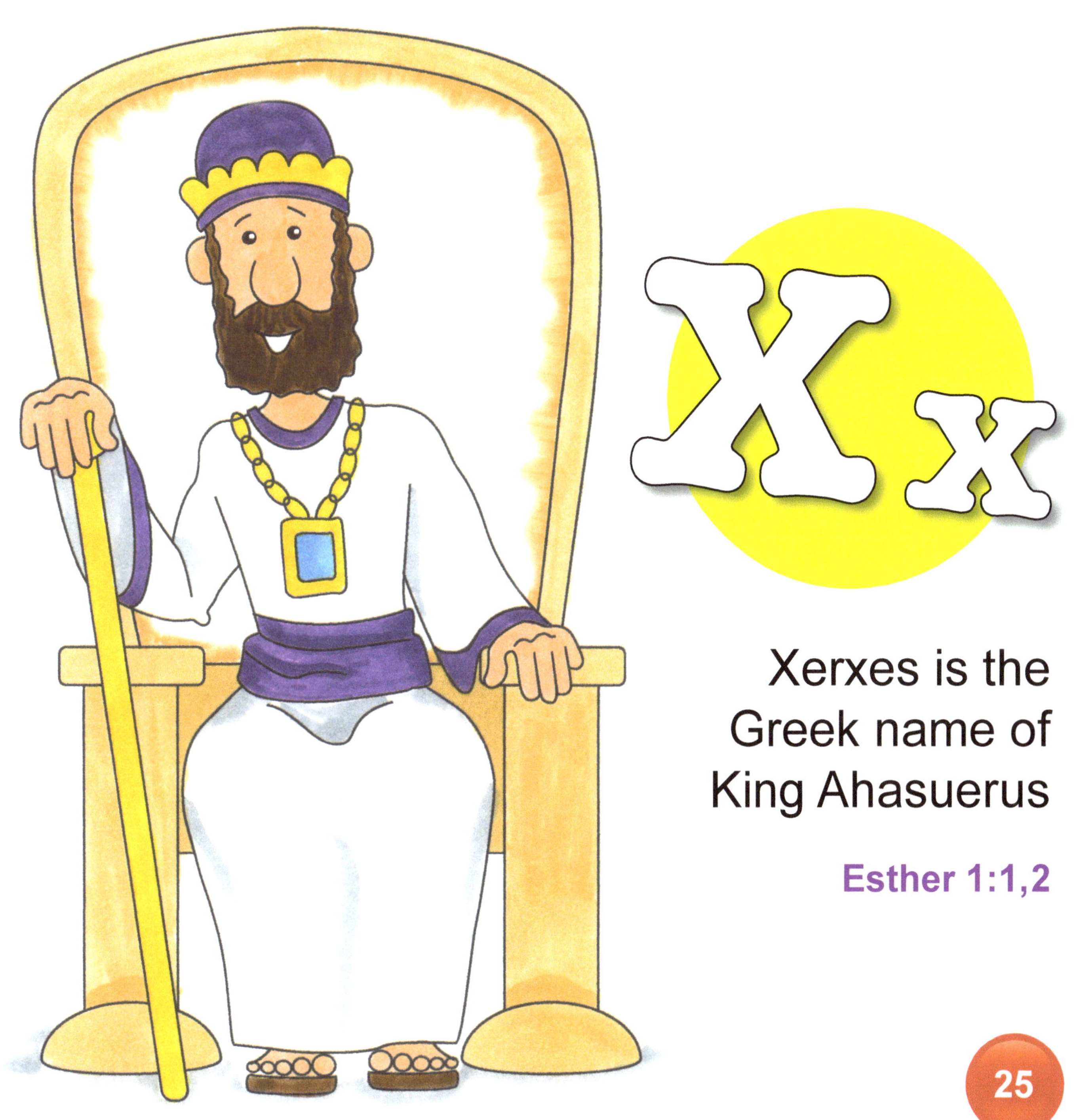

Xx

Xerxes is the
Greek name of
King Ahasuerus

Esther 1:1,2

25

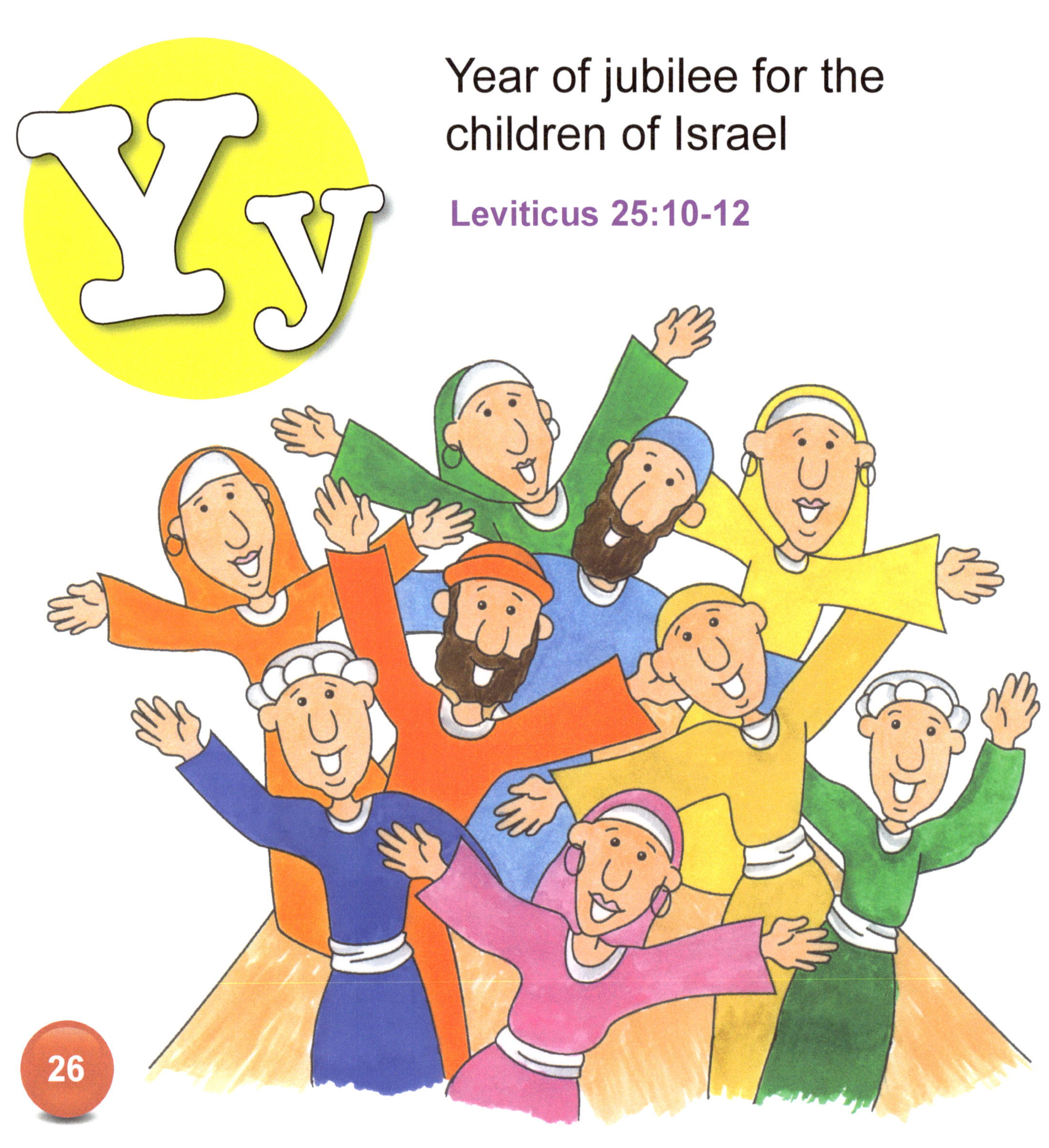

Year of jubilee for the
children of Israel

Leviticus 25:10-12

Z z
Zacchaeus in a tree
Luke 19:2-4
27